The Bear of Branston Cave
Jolyon G.C Stevenson

The Author

In 2013, Jolyon Stevenson enlisted in the Royal Navy and became a submariner. He left the military after ten years of service, making his career as a truck driver. In 2024, he finished his Level 4 Diploma in Editing and Proofreading alongside his driving role. During his time under the waves, he began writing multiple books, but he never finished any of them until early 2024. His mission to complete his unfinished novels is still ongoing, and the first one, 'The Bear of Branston Cave,' is now available. Inspired by his daughter Evalynn's love for animals, it was composed for her.

The Bear of Branston Cave
Jolyon G.C Stevenson

Dedications

I want to express my gratitude to my family for being there for me no matter what. This book is for everyone, but it is especially dedicated to my daughter, Evalynn. I apologise for the wait; I hope you find it enjoyable!

Contents

Cover

Author Page - **i**

Title Page

Copyright - **ii**

Dedications - **iii**

Contents - **iv**

The Bear of Branston Cave

Chapter 1 - Bryan of Branston Cave - **Page 1**

Chapter 2 - The Visitor - **Page 9**

Chapter 3 - Food For Thought - **Page 19**

Chapter 4 - The Journey Begins - **Page 27**

Chapter 5 - Return to the Farm - **Page 36**

Chapter 6 - Trouble in the Barn - **Page 43**

Chapter 7 - Not Into the Woods Yet - **Page 50**

Chapter 8 - The Final Hunt - **Page 57**

Chapter 1
Bryan Of Branston Cave

1

Once upon a time, nestled in the depths of the magnificent Tongass forest in North America, there existed a place of extraordinary natural wonder and bliss. This magical place was located in the southeast of Alaska, inside the vast Tongass National Forest. The Tongass was the biggest national forest in the country, including around 17 million acres of unspoiled wilderness.

This location was breathtakingly beautiful. The scenery was dominated by massive elderly trees, some of which were hundreds of years old. With Sitka spruce, Western red cedar, and hemlock making up most of these gigantic trees, the surrounding forest was vibrant with emerald green, extending as far as the eye could see. The leaves on their branches filtered the sunlight that hit the woodland floor, creating a natural sanctuary. This vast and varied ecosystem, where numerous kinds of plant and animal life thrived, was a testimony to the force of nature. As you progressed deeper into the Tongass forest, you would encounter a radiant undergrowth composed of moss-covered rocks, ferns, and numerous types of wildflowers, which added vivid tones to the natural landscape. The air was filled with the pleasant fragrance of wild flowers and the earthy scent of damp soil, the forest floor was a living carpet. There was constantly the sound of water running, beautiful streams flowing over smooth river stones as they wound through the woodland, producing calming tunes. This beautiful forest contained a big lake which sparkled in the sun. All of its residents called it Lake Luna, and its pure waters mirrored the emerald green of the surrounding woodland. This was a haven for a wide variety of creatures, a place of peace and contemplation, and a mirror to the heavens above.

Nestled within the embrace of the forest, the lake was a priceless gem, providing a peaceful haven for the species that made it home as well as any lucky tourists who happened to stumble across its shores. The sun's rays would shine on the lake's waters with golden dancing reflections, and the gentle touch of a cooling wind would frequently form ripples on the surface. Circling the lake were unspoiled old stands of trees that appeared to be the protectors of this marvel of nature, towering above the ground with their roots firmly ingrained in the rich soil. The majesty and beauty of the natural world were demonstrated by this little-known treasure in the middle of the Tongass forest. It was a place to retreat from the stress of modern-day life and find comfort in the peaceful embrace of the natural world. In this faraway part of North America, beauty and peace often went hand in hand to make a permanent haven for those who were lucky enough to experience it. Nestled not far from the glittering shores of Lake Luna, this enchanting realm concealed a wonderous cavern called Branston Cave. Within the dark recesses of this cavern, where the harmonies of eerie forest sounds echoed through the chambers, amidst the chorus of creepy crawly creatures, dwelled a majestic presence. It was Bryan, the grizzly bear, an intimidating figure.

Bryan appreciated the beauty of the forest and

occasionally delighted in the comforting warmth of the sun, but he had a fondness for going on night-time adventures in search of food and sustenance under the cover of darkness. He would hunt and forage all night long, then hide up in Branston Cave for protection. There, he would store his bounty and feast on it. He would usually fill up to the brim around daybreak, at which point he would curl up in a blissful sleep that lasted for several hours. Of everything that had ever touched his tongue, nothing compared to his favourite fresh salmon.

Bryan's exceptional ability to catch these quick-witted fish demonstrated his mastery of the hunt. But he also enjoyed foraging for wild berries, their luscious sweetness providing a welcome diversion from his usual meatier appetite. Bryan, however, was a solitary creature, deprived of the comforting presence of his mother for several years. Her untimely death had left a huge emptiness in his heart. Even more mysterious was the disappearance of his father during one of the coldest winters, leaving behind unanswered questions and a lingering sense of loss. Bryan's father had been the stuff of tales, a legendary grizzly bear known for his leadership abilities. Bryan listened to his mother's amazing stories about his father's adventures with wide eyes, enthralled by her storytelling.

One such extraordinary tale was the epic battle with a monstrous alligator, which became a legendary moment in grizzly bear history. A confrontation that had etched itself into the books of grizzly bear lore. The story began with Bryan's father returning from a successful hunt over a treacherous swamp. Suddenly, a gigantic alligator emerged from the depths, driven by a strong desire to steal the fruits of the grizzly bear's labour.

Undaunted, and despite the perilous odds, Bryan's wise father bravely battled the powerful reptile with an unwavering resolution and pure willpower. The usually peaceful area became disturbed by the crashing and splashing of the two giant opponents.

With relentless aggression, he grappled with the formidable reptile, skilfully manoeuvring to take the upper hand. Seizing an advantageous position, he employed a masterful sleeper hold. Once locked in, he subdued the alligator and rendered it powerless within minutes. The remaining alligators turned and ran away. Gripped by profound fear, they dared not cross his path as he traversed the rest of the swamp with his hard-earned food. That day he left his mark on the hearts of creatures, both close and far, forever etching his name into Tongass history.

But Bryan's life was shaped by more than simply his father's incredible stories. His mother was highly regarded for her generosity and readiness to lend a supporting paw to other animals in need. She was a kind and sympathetic bear with a heart of gold. She hunted not just to feed herself, but out of a selfless desire to support her darling son. Bryan learned many great lessons from his parents and was blessed with a unique combination of his father's power and prowess and his mother's compassionate and understanding disposition.

Bryan developed into a master hunter, honing his senses to become an unmatched fisherman and skilfully harvesting salmon away from their watery home. His strong sense of smell made him a powerful provider, not only for himself but for whatever number of bears he might have chosen to share his abundant food with. He was able to locate elusive rodents and find hidden caches of fruit. Bryan's creativity inside his cave produced an abundance of new food, demonstrating his proficiency in the outdoors and his steadfast dedication to surviving. He was a skilled hunter, as evidenced by the careful maintenance of the larder, which kept him fed even during the worst of circumstances. And so Bryan the grizzly bear, with his brave heart and skill, flourished in the domain of the great forest. He wandered the lush fields, his presence a symbol of power and kindness. Under his vigilant eye, the forest thrived, with creatures of all shapes and sizes finding comfort in his noble company. With each stride he took, the sound of nature resonated, and the animals of the forest mumbled his name in awe, their hearts overflowing with appreciation for his magnificent existence.

Bryan stood tall in the enormous forest, a symbol of kindness and resiliency, a picture of what it meant to be a grizzly bear. Bryan's shape disappeared into the forest as the sun sank below the horizon, bathing the peaceful woodland in a golden glow.

He was eager to go on another exciting adventure and leave his mark on the enchanted story of the forest.

Chapter 2
The Visitor

2

One night while the moon shone magnificently over the forest, Bryan the powerful grizzly bear, came back to his cave. He held a tiny berry tree in one hand and his favourite salmon in the other. His senses were filled with the comforting smell of his cave, but there was something unfamiliar in the air. Bryan noticed something off-putting in the darkness, it was a strange smell. He was intrigued and took two deep sniffs at the air, his sharp sense of smell searching hard to find the source.

He wrinkled his nose. "That's odd, I've never smelt that smell before."

Bryan followed the heavier aroma within his cave as his curiosity led him deeper and deeper. Out of nowhere, he heard his food corner's distinctive sound of scoffing and chewing. Feeling both surprised and irritated, he cleared his throat and prepared to face the invader.

Bryan bellowed, his powerful voice sent echoing across the cavern, "Who goes there? This is my cave and my food, so you had better not be stealing!"

He was shocked to see an animal he had never

seen before as a small head appeared. It was a pig, contently nibbling on his prized salmon. Bryan's anger softened as he took in the sight of the lost creature.

The pig, with a mouthful of salmon, muttered, "Sorry there, Mr. I didn't know this was your food. I've been lost from my family and have been searching for food for two whole days."

Bryan pondered what it might be like to go without food for such a long amount of time, his heart heavy with empathy.

Recognising the pig's situation, Bryan's face became sympathetic. "Oh, that's terrible. You can have some, but you must help me collect some more food tomorrow."

The pig finished his mouthful and then forced a smile as his eyes became wide with appreciation. "Oh, thank you so much, Mr...."

"Call me Bryan," the bear responded, offering a kind paw.

The little pig raised his trotter and they shook hands. Curious about the origins of his newfound friend, Bryan enquired, "What sort of animal are you, and what do you like to be called?"

"Thanks, Bryan. I'm what those weird human things call a pig, and my name is Paulo."

He proceeded to recount his tale of wandering from the farm where he lived with his siblings, getting lost in the forest, and stumbling upon Bryan's cave. Bryan listened intently as Paulo told his tale, understanding the pig's downfalls and the bravery required for him to survive on his own. They realised they had a lot of common interests and morals. A sense of brotherly respect began to form between the unlikely pair. Paulo, who was a little afraid of the dark, took comfort in Bryan's presence, and the bear relished the chance to mentor and teach his new friend.

They decided to set out at sunrise the next morning, embarking on an adventure to collect food. Bryan named his little bag of berries and seeds

'Super Bait', and the duo headed out of the cave. Bryan, acting as Paulo's mentor, led the way to Lake Luna, his favourite fishing spot. Bryan shared his wisdom of the forest with Paulo as they travelled, warning him about alligators in Kangorn Swamp and mountain lions in North Rock, among other possible threats. Paulo was grateful for Bryan's leadership and was amazed at the bear's extensive local knowledge. Bryan's curiosity took over and he asked Paulo about his life on the farm. Paulo excitedly talked about his adventures, describing the variety of animals he lived with and the pig pen. He gave an explanation of the idea behind farmers, one of those peculiar human things who wore materials and hats and used those telephone gadgets to take pictures of themselves, a practice known as selfies. Bryan nodded, remembering times when people carried metal sticks that banged loudly and hurt animals. But he also noted the humans who strolled around the forest in peace, taking pictures of their moments using devices resembling those Paulo described. Bryan's keen sense of smell allowed him to detect the humans well enough to be able to identify them from a distance. He watched the people warily, being both curious and respectful of their presence. The two friends grew to deeply admire each other as their chat went on. Paulo valued Bryan's strength and dignity, and Bryan valued Paulo's cheerful attitude and devotion, which were qualities uncommon in the animal kingdom.

Arriving at Lake Luna, Bryan proudly showed the stunning view to Paulo. The pig was visibly excited as he stared in awe at the area's beauty and vibrancy. Bryan gave Paulo a rundown of his fishing methods, deciding to start at the top ledge where the salmon would jump up and provide an easy catch. Paulo took his place on the ledge where Bryan suggested, and then Bryan made his way to the base of the waterfall. With great anticipation, they readied their 'Super Bait'. They then waited, anticipation filling the air. Within moments, the water came alive with a frenzy of activity as salmon leapt from the lake and tumbled down the waterfall. Paulo was thrilled and amazed at the sight in front of him. With big wide eyes, his mouth hung open in awe. Bryan demonstrated his technique. Effortlessly, he scooped a jumping fish out of the air and caught it in his mouth.

Paulo prepared himself and, motivated by his friend's display, got into position to capture a salmon of his own. A salmon flew into the air, and Paulo leapt quickly to catch it, his lips shutting around the juicy catch. The little pig's sheer joy caused him to tumble down the waterfall, making a huge splash.

Bryan hurriedly looked over the edge at the water where Paulo had just disappeared. "Paulo!!"
A few moments passed and nothing. Bryan just about to jump in and rescue his new friend, was relieved as Paulo popped back up to the surface with the salmon still in his mouth.

Bryan's initial concern quickly turned into pride. "Well done, Paulo, brilliant!"

They caught several more salmon together and

set them down by the lakeside. They splashed around in the water, having a good time as they celebrated their catch and their newfound friendship. Feeling the rumbles of hunger in their bellies, they each gulped down a recently caught salmon, relishing the reward of their hard work. After gathering the last of the fish, they returned to Bryan's cave, eager to unwind and have a bigger meal.

Paulo turned to Bryan, his gratitude shining in his eyes, "Thank you, Bryan. That was the most fun I've ever had."

Bryan grinned broadly, happy with their success. "That's no problem at all, Paulo. You owed me some salmon, and you have repaid me well. Plus, you've learned how to fish, and it turns out you're a natural."

Paulo smiled at the praise, grateful for the friendship and the wisdom that Bryan shared. Just as Bryan and Paulo were talking about their plans for the next day, a sudden and threatening growl echoed through the forest. The two companions froze, alarm spreading across their faces. An animal with menacing yellow eyes, appeared from the dense trees before them, snarling.

Bryan let out a startled "Ahhh!" and dropped part of the salmon he was holding. He fumbled, shocked by the close danger. He was momentarily on edge, but he calmed down quickly and concentrated on defending his friend. "It's a wolf, Paulo, stay back!"

The wolf's menacing gaze fixated on them as it stepped forward and stopped in front of them. "Who are you?"

Bryan grabbed the initiative and moved forward cautiously. "I'm Bryan the Grizzly Bear, and this is Paulo the Pig. We don't want any trouble, we're just passing through."

The wolf glanced from Paulo to Bryan, examining them closely. There was a hint of wonder and curiosity in her voice. "What a strange pair to find in the woods."

Bryan, managing to keep calm and composed, looked the wolf in the eyes. "And what's your name?"

"My name is Dera the Wolf. I will not harm you, but I will ask if I could take one of those fish. I lost my pack somewhere along the creek, and it's been a lot harder to hunt on my own."

Paulo showed Dera his kindness. He stepped forward slowly and put a salmon down in front of her. "You can have one I caught."

"Thank you, Paulo," Dera responded, her voice becoming softer. She continued toward the salmon, flashing her sharp, pearly teeth. "You seem like you know how to provide for a girl. I'm glad I didn't eat you now."

Paulo gulped and although his anxiety showed, he looked Dera in the eyes. "That's... alright. I lost my family too, so I hope you ma... manage to find yours."

Dera looked at Paulo, still showcasing her sharp teeth. She spoke with gratitude. "Oh, I will."
Saying no more, Dera stepped forward and collected the fish. She then turned and vanished into the trees.

Paulo, still shaking from the experience, looked at

Bryan "Well, that was a bit scary."

Bryan put his hand on Paulo's shoulder "You did well there, Paulo. That could have easily gone another way. Wolves can be dangerous, especially when there's a whole pack. I've had to fight them before. But, she seemed to like you."

Paulo joked, "Well, I guess that's because I got the best charm from the farm," which caused them both to burst out laughing, happy that they had not been harmed.

Paulo thought about the excitement and danger of their encounter with Dera as they made their way back to the cave.

After arriving safely, they stored the fish away and made themselves comfortable for the night so they could recover and get ready for the adventures ahead.

Chapter 3
Food For Thought

3

Bryan woke up the following morning feeling the warmth of the morning embrace as the sun rose higher in the sky, creating a dazzling display of colours. He nudged Paulo gently out of his sleep, the pig blinking away the last of his dreams to be met with the sight of a breakfast feast spread in front of him. Under the sun, salmon gleamed along with a variety of mackerel, crisp veggies, and juicy fruits.

Bryan smiled with a warmth that matched the sunrise. "Bon appétit."

Paulo looked at the spread in front of him, his eyes widening with joy. "Wow, Bryan, this is incredible. Thank you."

Bryan smiled, clearly pleased to see his friend enjoying the food. They consumed their food leisurely, relishing every bite until their stomachs felt full. They sighed in satisfaction. Bryan let out a hearty burp, then grinned happily and rested his hands on his belly. "That was divine."

Paulo, his gut stuffed full, nodded slightly. "That was absolutely delicious."

Bryan's eyes strayed to the delicious leftovers on their plates as they enjoyed the glow of the warm fire. A memorable smile appeared on his face. "You know, Paulo, this feast reminds me of the meals my mother used to prepare when I was just a cub." Paulo leaned in carefully, listening attentively. "Really? Tell me about it, Bryan."

Bryan started telling his story, memories shining in his eyes. "My mother was an exceptional cook. She had a way of turning the simplest ingredients into the most delicious dishes. One of my favourites was her honey-glazed salmon. She would catch the freshest fish from the river, marinate it in a special blend of herbs and spices, and then glaze it with honey harvested from nearby beehives."

Paulo's mouth watered at the description. " Wow, that sounds incredible. Did she cook anything else?"

"A lot," Bryan laughed in response. "There were her famous berry pies, made with wild berries she picked herself. And her vegetable stew, filled with hearty root vegetables which simmered for hours over the fire until it was bursting with flavour."

Paulo hung on to everything Bryan said. "She sounds like an amazing cook."

Bryan smiled, remembering his mother. "She was, but more than that, she was an amazing mother. She taught me a great deal of things that I now realise were valuable life lessons. Her knowledge was second to none. Everything I know about cooking, survival in the wild, hunting and fishing, along with foraging for food, was mostly down to her. And she always made sure our bellies were full and our hearts were warm."

Bryan smiled mournfully, remembering how much his mother had loved and cared for him. "I miss her every day, but whenever I cook a meal like this, I feel like she's right here with me, guiding my paw."

Paulo felt a surge of sympathy for his friend. "I'm sorry for your loss, Bryan. But I'm glad you have those memories to hold onto."

Bryan gave a nod, his eyes full of gratitude. "Thank you, Paulo. And who knows, maybe one day I'll teach you some of her recipes. I'm sure you'd make a fine chef yourself."

Paulo grinned at the idea, feeling grateful for Bryan's offer. "I'd like that, Bryan. But for now, I think I'll just enjoy the meals you prepare for us."

They smiled at each other and leaned back, enjoying the warmth of their friendship.

As the sun rose higher in the sky, shining on them with its golden beams, they realised that they would always have that friendship, regardless of the experiences that were ahead of them.

Again, Bryan's gaze fixed on Paulo. "So, what I was saying last night before you fell asleep, was that I would help you retrace your steps if you like, so you can find your way home to your family."

Paulo's eyes brightened with relief and thanks. "Oh, that's so kind of you Bryan. Thank you so much."

Bryan's smile faded and this time he looked more seriously at Paulo. "And just so you know, if we can't find the way back, you are always welcome to stay here with me for as long as you like. There's plenty of room."

Paulo seemed liberated in his response, "Thanks, Bryan. I think I would actually prefer that. After being stuck on that farm all my life, I feel so invigorated and much more alive here with you than I ever have in the confines of that awful pig pen. But I would like to head back so I can let my brothers and sisters know that I'm safe and that they don't need to worry. I will also let them know that there is more to life than just surviving as a prisoner there. I believe they will all want to leave and come with me."

Bryan's eyes glistened with acceptance and understanding. "They are more than welcome to stay here too, as long as they chip in with the food collecting. There's plenty of room for everyone."

Paulo yelled with delight, "Awesome, let's break them free then!"

Bryan turned to Paulo. "Right then, we'll make a plan, gather some more supplies, and head off early tomorrow."

Their unwavering determination set the stage for their upcoming mission. They discussed their plans in more detail.

Bryan looked deep in thought. "I think we should

try this rescue in the evening when there will be fewer humans and animals about."

Paulo liked Bryan's way of thinking. "Yes, I agree."

Bryan wondered about security, "So, what sort of alarm systems do they have at the farm?"

"No alarms that I can think of. At least not in the pig pen. But there is a guard dog named Bruce. He usually helps the farmer round up the sheep. He can be a bit mean sometimes as he once bit one of my brothers when they strayed from the pen. He probably would have bitten me the night I left, but I think he was asleep in the farmer's house. Also, there's the farmer, who is usually inside the farmhouse by sundown."

"OK, Paulo, I will deal with Bruce. I'll try to handle it peacefully, maybe lure him with food while you sneak into the barn and open the gate to free your brothers and sisters. If that doesn't work, we'll resort to plan B and try to trap him somewhere while we make our escape. If the farmer is in the house, then this should be a fairly straightforward mission. How far is it from the edge of the forest to the farm?"

Paulo responded with animated trotter tapping that resembled playing a piano. "About 500 pig steps."

"Alright then Paulo, now we need to figure out how many pig steps are equal to one bear step, so we can calculate."

They experimented with their steps as they made their way up and down the cave until they arrived at a decision.

Paulo sat down. "So, using our formula, five pig steps are equal to one bear step. That means 500 pig steps would be 100 bear steps."

Bryan confirmed as their strategy slowly began to take shape, "Okay, so it's 100 bear steps from the edge of the forest to the farm."

The day went on with talks, plans, and a strong feeling of anticipation. The journey ahead drew them in, offering a path of self-discovery, resilience, and the unshakable bond between Bryan the Grizzly Bear and Paulo the Pig. Once the plans were confirmed, they worked out what items they would need for their mission. They gathered supplies and food and arranged them neatly next to their beds, ready to go on their journey as soon as the sun rose. Paulo's eyes had already grown heavy and started to close.

He turned to Bryan. "Goodnight, Bryan."

A warm smile played on Bryan's lips. "Good night, buddy."

Within minutes, the two friends gave in to the call of sleep and in the cave's silence, they slept peacefully. Their dreams from that night were of the enduring power of their new friendship and the successes and challenges that lay ahead of them in the days to come.

Chapter 4
The Journey Begins

4

They got up early the next morning, bodies ready and spirits full of determination to face the trials that lay ahead. As they walked past Lake Luna, with its serene surface reflecting the soft light of dawn, they thought quickly back to the fish they had captured the day before. They set off again, their mission revitalized, and went around the other side of the lake and took a path leading deeper into the forest, more into it.

They strolled for hours, using Paulo's recollection as a guide through the deep jungle until they came to a clearing. Bryan's keen senses snapped to attention as he took in their surroundings.

Bryan stopped in his tracks, leant over to Paulo and whispered in his ear. "Be careful up ahead."

Paulo stopped as well. "Is there something there?" "That's Kangorn Swamp over there on the right, in other words, Alligator Central."

The very thought of alligators made Paulo's heart skip a beat. He took a moment and prepared himself for what might happen. "What's the plan?"

Bryan presented their plan, his brow wrinkled with

concentration. "We'll stick to the left-hand side, keeping our distance from the water and moving as quietly as possible. With any luck, none of them will notice us."

Paulo nodded, looking determined. "Okay, let's get started."

They moved forward carefully, the stillness of the swamp strange and unsettling. As they tiptoed passed the dark waters, Paulo couldn't get rid of the feeling that he was being watched. But just when they believed they were in the clear, Paulo heard a noise.

Paulo looked around, slowly moving closer to the sound. "What's that noise?" he whispered.

Bryan felt his muscles tighten as he followed Paulo's gaze. That's when they both realised what they were seeing. They were shocked and gasped for air. All around them, was the site of a dozen sleeping alligators all spread out and camouflaged. The alligators were completely unaware of their intruders.

Paulo pulled a tense face and spoke in a quiet whisper. "It must be their snoring we can hear."

Bryan murmured frantically, "No sudden movements, Paulo," his eyes darting between the sleeping reptiles.

They cautiously made their way past the sleeping predators, their hearts thumping in their chests as they went. However, just as they were about to reach the safety of the forest, Paulo let out an enormous burp, breaking the silence like a thunderclap.

"Burrrrrrrrrp!! Sorry, it's those berries we packed," Paulo explained defensively, his cheeks flushing with shame.

Their worst fears were realised as they turned to see the alligators stirring from their slumber, their hungry eyes fixed on the intruders in their territory.

Bryan yelled, "Ruuuun!" with a sense of urgency as he scooped up Paulo under his arm and propelled them into the forest with his powerful legs. They dashed through the undergrowth, the sound of chomping teeth and water splattering behind them, until at last they came to a quiet area where they could take a breather.

Bryan stopped to catch his breath and put Paulo down, relief shining across his face. "I think we lost them."

"I'm so glad," Paulo said, wiping sweat from his brow. "Sorry about the burp, but those berries make me a bit gassy."

Despite their situation, Bryan laughed, his eyes softening as he glanced at his friend. "It's okay, Paulo. We all have our moments. The important thing is that we made it through together."

As they walked, their thoughts were fixed on getting to their destination safely, even though their hearts were still pounding from the adrenaline high. While walking with unwavering determination through the dark woodland, Paulo remembered the route he had taken when he was lost.

They continued walking and eventually came to a bushy area that seemed suitable for setting up camp. After enjoying some of the salmon they had brought with them, they decided to take turns to keep watch. One of them would stay awake while the other one rested. They slept in shifts, alert to any danger that could be hiding in the shadows.

Refreshed and rested, they set out again in the morning. Paulo sensed that they were getting closer to the farm as they walked, the noises and sights of civilisation becoming more and more familiar with each mile.

Paulo turned to Bryan, looking both excited and nervous. "We're not too far from the farm now."

Bryan smiled but could see the clear worry on his friend's face. "Don't worry Paulo, everything will be fine. Just a few more fields to go hopefully."

They strolled on until Paulo stopped and pointed toward an ancient elm tree. "Here's the old elm tree. I used to sneak out the pen and come and lie here sometimes when I was having a bad day. It helped me relax. Maybe we should stop here quickly and have a snack?

"Sure, let's review our plan and have a snack. Also, we'll set this as our rendezvous location in case anything goes wrong."

Paulo looked puzzled. "What's a rendezvous?"
Bryan explained. "A rendezvous is a meeting point at an agreed time and place. In this case, it's where we'll meet either after completing our mission or if something goes wrong and we need to regroup."

Paulo munched some berries. "Oh, that's a good idea, Bryan."

Paulo then pulled out some apples they had saved for this occasion. He passed one to Bryan then crunched into one immediately, the crisp fruit providing a much-needed burst of flavour.

"Alright, Paulo," Bryan began, wiping the juice from his muzzle. "Let's go over the plan one more time. We need to make sure we're prepared for anything and everything."

Paulo nodded, his thoughts fixed on the mission at hand. "We'll head towards the property once it becomes dark. We need the keys to the barn, so we'll have to break into the farmer's house first. The farmer stores them somewhere right inside the front door. I am aware of this because I have heard them jingle when he walks, but whenever he goes through his front door and shuts it, they jingle for a couple of footsteps and then make one final jangle and then the footsteps continue. He must hang them up somewhere. Since I'm much smaller than you, I should try to slip in through the cat flap. Mittens, the farmer's cat, is a fish lover, you should have no issue luring him away. I can then slip in via the cat flap and get the keys after he's out of the picture. After that, I'll step outside to meet you, and together we'll head toward the barn to aid in my family's escape. Bruce, the dog, typically sleeps outside in the barn keeping watch over the animals, so we'll need to be careful not to wake him when we're close to the pen. I'll unlock the pen with the key we took earlier, and together, my siblings and I, will leave as quietly as possible. We'll exit the barn and move in the direction of the clearing where we had our meeting last evening. After that, we'll go back the way we came, being cautious to stay away from the dangers we faced on our journey here."

Bryan paid close attention, his appreciation for Paulo's detailed planning visible in his eyes. "Sounds like a solid plan Paulo. Remember that we must stay calm and focused."

Paulo looked worried, "But what if you get in trouble or if the farmer wakes up?"

Bryan grinned confidently. "Then I'll run even faster."

Paulo looked sternly at Bryan and confessed his concerns. "I'm not entirely sure about this, Bryan. It seems extremely dangerous. If anything happens to you, I'll never forgive myself."

Bryan cheerfully reassured Paulo, "Nonsense, Paulo. I'll be fine, and we'll be back at the cave with your family in no time."

Paulo pulled himself together, "Okay then, let's do this!"

"If something goes wrong, we adjust ourselves and find a different solution. Paulo, we are in this together."

Paulo grinned appreciatively as the burden of their joint mission eased with Bryan's wise words. "I couldn't ask for a better friend Bryan. Thank you for everything. I am so very grateful."

With their plan now firmly in mind, they settled down and took a seat beneath the oak tree. The excitement of what lay ahead blended with the peace of the forest around them. Before long, exhaustion had caught up with them, and they were fast asleep, having dreams of freedom and triumph.

Chapter 5
Return To The Farm

5

Paulo could hear his heart pounding in his chest as the two friends moved as stealthily as possible towards the farm, their determination mixed with a hint of fear and adrenaline pumping through their veins. As they got closer to the farmer's house, they peered through the darkness and saw that the lights were out.

Inside, the darkness seemed to swallow him whole as he slipped through the window, his massive frame moving with surprising grace. Bryan turned to face Paulo, who was still outside the open window looking up at him eagerly. He then reached out carefully, grabbed the little pig and pulled him inside. The farmer's cat, Mittens, suddenly appeared from the darkness and made a low growl toward the unlikely pair.

Bryan responded to the danger and pulled out a nice juicy fresh salmon," Stick to the plan, Paulo."

"Here kitty kitty," Bryan urged, waving the fish towards the window as he went back outside.

Mittens was powerless to refuse such a tasty offering. He followed the dangling salmon while purring with big hungry eyes. He then hopped onto the windowsill and followed Bryan and the salmon outside.

Meanwhile, inside, Paulo moved through the unfamiliar surroundings on tiptoe. His senses were on high alert as the darkness shrouded him like a cloak and his trotters barely made a sound on the wooden floorboards.

As Paulo walked around a corner, he spotted the keys hanging by the front door. Since height was not on his side, he quietly dragged a small wooden stool into place, climbed up, and took the keys. He then took the keys and climbed back out the window, this time carefully closing it on his way out.

Meanwhile, Bryan encountered another problem outside. Bryan coaxed Mittens into a clearing close to the edge of a nearby field. He dropped the salmon for the ecstatic Mittens who finally had his reward.

He backed away as the cat started to devour the tasty treat. "Enjoy it Mittens, and just so you know, there is more where that came from." Bryan turned back to the farm and added, "I will be back soon with more if you wait right here."

However, just as Mittens became distracted, a different animal appeared.

The animal cleared its throat, "Hut-hum, excuse me there, Mr. Bear, is it? I'm Kevin, the Cockerel. Do you mind explaining to me why a grizzly bear is on the property of the house of my owner, Mr. Bonsworth, the farmer?"

"Well," Bryan paused for a moment to think, "what happened is I was chasing a mouse, and I think it got into that house back there. So, I was peering through the window to see if it was there, but I must have lost it. But since it's not, I'll be on my way now. See ya," Bryan said, half turning away.

"Whoa, not so fast, Beeeaaar," declared Kevin the Cockerel. "Not only am I the morning alarm at 'o' seven hundred sharp, but I also raise the alarm if any unwelcome intruders are on the premises.

And you, Mr. Bear, are on the premises and looking shifty. So, without further ado..."

The Cockerel took a deep breath, about to wake up the whole farm.

Bryan, though, moved fast. He snatched the surprised Kevin by the beak to stop him from squawking or screaming. After making a quick dash back to the clearing, he used slender branches and twigs to tie his beak closed.

"I'm sorry, Kevin, but you left me no choice. I will untie you as soon as I have explained my situation. If you decide you want to wake the whole farm up then so be it, but please listen to what I am about to tell you. My friend Paulo the Pig, who you probably know, got separated from his family who live here in the barn. While lost, Paulo travelled for three days through a vast and dangerous forest and ended up starving and looking for food in my cave. After meeting Paulo and getting to know him I found out that he is a very brave and loyal animal. He explained to me how he was lost from his family who were entrapped here and ruled with an iron fist by a creature known as Bruce the dog and his owner the farmer. I offered Paulo a permanent home in my cave along with his family and vowed, as his friend, to help him reunite with them and help them escape from their captivity and live with me in freedom, living a full and happy natural life like all animals should. Together me and Paulo came up with a plan and travelled three days back here to rescue his family. Surely Kevin, you can find it in yourself to understand and even help us rescue his family. There's plenty of room in my cave and also plenty of salmon for everyone. Even you are welcome to join us. I'm going to untie you now that I have explained my reasons for the intrusion, and I hope you can find it in your heart to forgive me for getting off on the wrong foot and also join us on our quest for freedom."

Bryan's fingers were shaking as he untied Kevin's beak. His heart was pounding in his chest as he awaited the cockerel's response. As a single tear rolled down Kevin's feathery cheek, Bryan felt a surge of hope swell within him.

"Mr Bryan, after carefully listening to your heroic adventure which has brought a tear to my eye, I can absolutely say with all my heart that not only am I moved by your story but truly honoured that you would offer me a wonderful life of freedom with you, Mr Paulo and his family. I've been a solitary bird ever since my mum passed away when I was a young cockerel and as soon as you mentioned family, I felt a huge connection to your cause. Not only will I help you in your mission, but I will join you in your habitat. I've had enough of that Bruce the dog pushing his weight around anyway."

Bryan felt a wave of relief as he heard Kevin's words, his heart bursting with happiness and thanks. With a shaky voice, he mustered, "Thank you, Kevin. Together, we will make a difference. Together, we will bring freedom to those who have been imprisoned for too long."

Now friends, they turned around and made their way back to the farm, where they reunited with

Paulo.

Paulo was not expecting Kevin at Bryan's side and looked confused "Bryan you made it, and I see you've met Kevin. How have you been Kevin?"

"Hello Paulo, it has been a while my friend. It is really good to see you again. I have heard great things about you from Bryan and I'm pleased to tell you that I will be joining you both on your quest."

Paulo was so happy he hopped with excitement "Yeesss, nice one Kevin, Thanks!"

Kevin looked respectfully at Paulo "The honour is all mine."

Bryan smiled. "The more the merrier."
Paulo turned towards the direction of the barn "Let's go, guys!"

They headed for the barn with a fresh sense of purpose. Their hearts raced as they got ready to take on whatever obstacles were in their way.

Chapter 6
Trouble In The Barn

6

Bryan, Paulo and Kevin quietly made their way to the barn, carefully avoiding any stray twigs or loose rocks that might give away their presence.

Paulo cautiously approached the door, his trotters barely making a sound. "I'll go ahead guys, give it a few minutes and follow me in."

Paulo took a deep breath and reached out to test the door, feeling glad that it was unlocked. He carefully pulled open the door and looked inside to make sure the coast was clear. The barn was dimly lit by a single lantern, throwing lengthy shadows over the hay-covered ground. The leathery smell of old barn board and fresh wood chips was strong as he stepped inside.

Paulo's eyes scanned the inside, trying to find any indication of Bruce the dog. Paulo sighed in relief as he saw the dog's sleeping shape close to the back of the barn.

With careful steps, he made his way towards the pen where his siblings were sleeping. He approached the pen containing his brothers with cautious strides, the keys clenched in his hoof.

"Wakey wakey, guys! It's me, Paulo," he called out. Four little faces looked up in shock.

Peter looked up in disbelief. "Paulo, is that really you?"

Patrick smiled at Paulo "We thought we'd never see you again!"

Penny looked sincere. "I thought you were dead," "I knew you'd be back!" shouted Patricia with joy.

Peter butted back in. "Where have you been Paulo?"

"It's a long story, but I've been on an adventure and met a bear. He's invited us all to live in his cave. So, I'm here to break you out!" Paulo explained.

"A cave? That sounds spooky," said Patrick sceptically.

"How far is it?" asked Peter.

"Will there be enough space for us?" inquired Patricia.

Penny looked worried. "Will we be safe?"

Paulo inhaled deeply, catching his breath before answering their questions. "It's not spooky at all. It's warm, and there's a beautiful lake nearby with tasty fish. It's a two-day walk away, with a sleep in the middle. We won't die; we know the route well, and we have a bear with us. So, what do you say brothers and sisters? Do you want to join me?"

Penny spoke first. "It's a definite yes from me. It's really so boring here I could die."

Patrick smiled and nodded. "Okay, I'm in."
Peter spoke next. "I'm in too,"

Patricia put her hands on her hips. "Well, I'm not going to stay here on my own, and it does sound rather exciting. So, on that note, I'm also in."

"You're not going anywhere!" a gruff voice interrupted them from behind.

When Paulo turned around, he was confronted by Bruce the dog, baring his fangs and snarling. "Get back in your pen immediately, piggy," Bruce commanded pointing at the pig pen.

Paulo was defiant and angry. "I will not! Me and my family don't want to stay here anymore. We're leaving tonight!"

"You know what happened to the last pig that crossed me, don't you?" Bruce threatened.

Paulo faced Bruce with unwavering determination, his heart thumping in his chest as he stood his ground. For the first time ever, he was taking on the powerful dog that had dominated the barn with an iron paw.

Bryan and Kevin walked in and stood at Paulo's side. Their presence gave Paulo even more strength and courage.

Paulo looked Bruce right in the eyes. "We are not afraid of you, Bruce. You can't keep us here forever. We deserve to be free. We're leaving, and there's nothing you can do to stop us!"

Bruce's growls became louder with every step as he moved closer to Paulo, his eyes narrowing into slits.

However, Bryan stepped forward, his massive frame towering over the dog. "Enough, Bruce," Bryan's voice rumbled like distant thunder. "You have held these pigs captive for too long. It's time to let them go."

Kevin spoke up, his voice heavy with authority, "You heard him, Bruce. They're leaving, and you're not going to stand in their way."

Bruce hesitated for a moment, his gaze flickering between the bear, the cockerel and the determined pig in front of him. For the first time, doubt crept into his eyes, uncertainty clouding his usual air of dominance. Bruce's confidence was starting to diminish.

"Who do you think you are bear? This is my territory, and I'll do whatever it takes to protect it."

Bryan returned Bruce's stare with unwavering determination in his eyes. "Simply put, I'm just a bear who believes in doing what is right. And right now, what's right is letting Paulo and his family go free."

It looked for a moment as though Bruce the dog would give in. But then suddenly, with his teeth bared and claws extended he surged forward with a snarl of frustration.

In a blur of movement, Bryan and Kevin leapt into action, intercepting Bruce with lightning speed. With a loud thud, the three animals collided. Then they rolled and tumbled across the barn floor in a flurry of fists and paws, sending fur and feathers flying.

Paulo took advantage of the distraction and got his siblings out of the pig pen. He pointed to the open door. "Come on, let's go!"

Paulo led the pigs as they left the barn, venturing outside into the refreshing night air and escaping the tension of their captivity. Paulo felt both fear and excitement in his heart as they dashed across the fields toward their rendezvous point at the clearing. At last, they were free.

Behind them, the barn door creaked shut with a loud bang. But Paulo with the responsibility of getting his family to safety, didn't look back.

The beautiful glow of the moon overhead welcomed them as they emerged into the clearing, its mellow light giving the surrounding forest a silvery sheen. Bryan, Kevin and Bruce continued their fierce struggle inside the barn, the sound of their clash echoing through the night.

Paulo stopped walking and turned to face his

siblings. "Let's hold position here and wait for them. I know they will make it."

Chapter 7
Not Into The Woods Yet

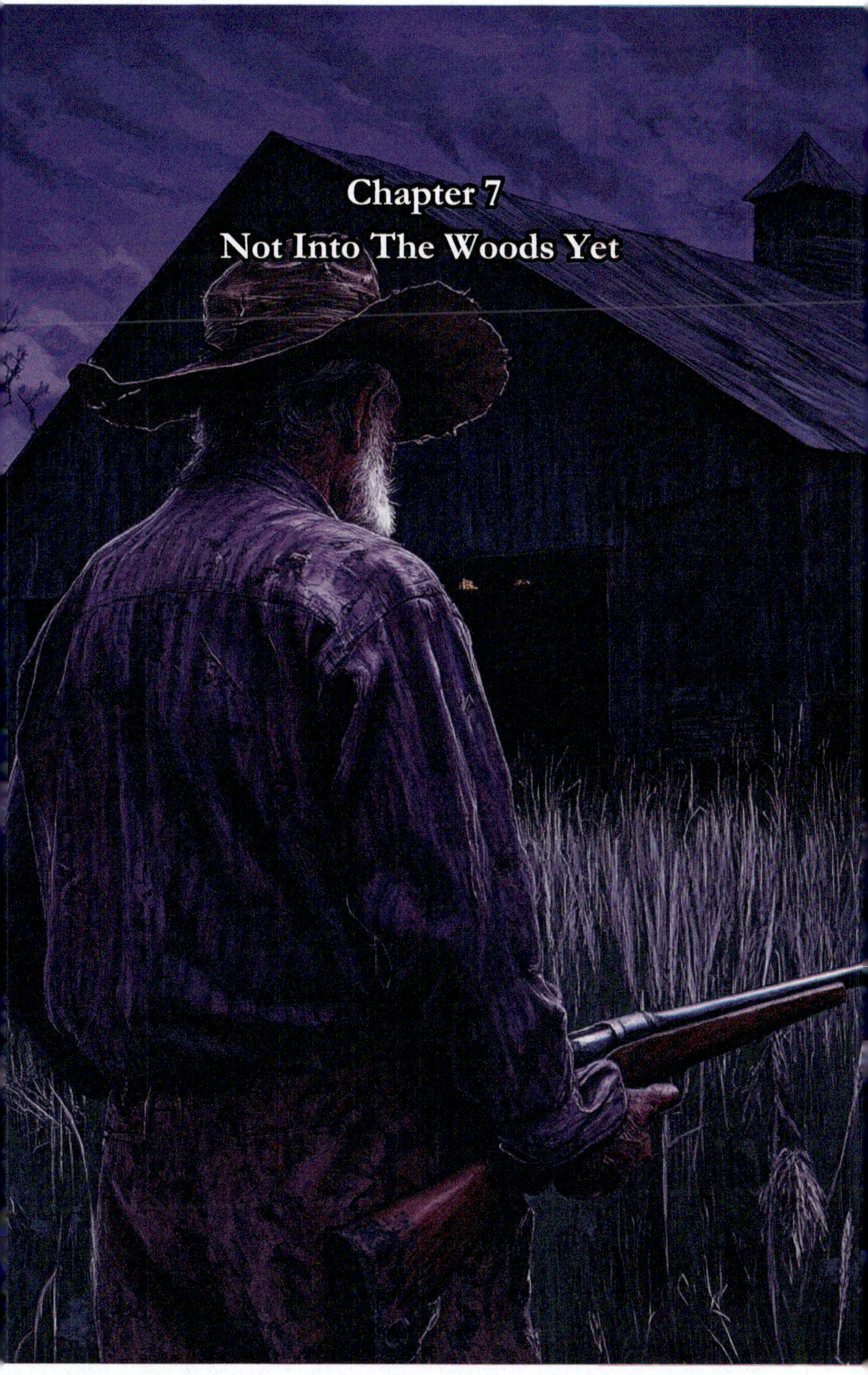

7

As they waited in the clearing, Paulo and his siblings huddled close together to keep warm. Their hearts were still racing from their daring escape. The tension in the air was thick as they strained to hear any sound of their friends emerging from the barn.

Suddenly, a loud noise shattered the stillness of the night. 'BANG!!'
The booming sound echoed through the clearing, causing Paulo and his siblings to jump in surprise.

"What was that?" Penny squealed, her eyes wide with fright.

Paulo's ears twitched as he attempted to listen. "I'm not sure," he admitted, his voice sounding worried. "But it sounds like trouble. We need to go back for our friends. Follow me quickly and keep quiet."

Mr Bonsworth, the farmer, stood at his closed barn door reloading his shotgun. He was stood there wearing his floppy old hunting hat, faded pyjamas with holes in and old wellies that were longing to be replaced. His teeth were chattering slightly and the mist of his breath was visible when he spoke. "That was just a warning shot!" he declared. "The next one is gonna hurt summin' awful!" he threatened.

He then pressed his ear against the door and continued to threaten his unknown intruders. "Now I'm going to open this door and y'all better come out with your hands raised, or I'm gonna start shooting!"

Paulo and his siblings were just out of sight but they could see the farmer from behind as he stood at the barn door with his shotgun in hand. Paulo's heart sank as he heard the farmer's threats. They were so close to freedom, yet now they faced the very real danger of being caught and returned to captivity or worse. He exchanged worried glances with his siblings, their eyes reflecting the fear and uncertainty that gnawed at their hearts.

Patricia was trembling with terror as she whispered to Paulo. "We can't let him catch us."

Paulo nodded, his mind racing as he thought of a way out of their troubled situation. He had to think fast if they were to help Bryan and Kevin make it out of the barn safely and escape the farmer's wrath.

With a sense of urgency, Paulo quickly formulated a plan. His eyes lit up when he finally came up with an idea. "I need to distract the farmer," he whispered to his siblings, his voice low but determined. "While he's focused on me, Bryan and Kevin might have a chance to slip out the back of the barn."

Patricia's eyes were wide with concern. "But won't that put you in danger Paulo?"

Paulo nodded, acknowledging the risk. "It's a risk," he admitted. "But it's our best chance to help Bryan and Kevin escape. If it wasn't for Bryan, I don't know where I would be. But I wouldn't be here being able to set us all free. I owe him a lot. We all do. Wait here and I will be back. I love you all." said Paulo.

Peter looked up and wished his brother on. "Good luck Paulo, you've got this."

Patrick spoke with certainty. "I know you can do this."

"We believe in you!" said Patricia convinced.

Penny looked him right in the eyes. "Good luck bro,

don't die!"

With a determined nod and added confidence Paulo left his siblings at the clearing and crept towards the barn. His heart was pounding in his chest as he approached. He knew he had to act fast if he wanted to create a big enough distraction to buy his friends time to escape. He saw Mr Bonsworth with his shotgun ready, standing close to the barn.

Unaware that the pig was behind him, Bonsworth carried on talking to whoever was in his barn. "Right, that's it, I've given warning, now I'm coming in!" declared Bonsworth as he booted open the barn door with his foot.

In an instant, and out of desperation, Paulo flung the closest object he could find at Mr. Bonsworth. It happened to be an old damp and chewed-on carrot that struck the farmer on the back of the head with a light thud.

Bonsworth was shocked as the cold, wet vegetable slapped off the back of his head. "Huh, what the devil was that?"

Bonsworth turned to see the carrot and then Paulo. He was furious when he worked out what had happened. "What are you doing out of your cage Pig!?" He drew his gun on Paulo. Just then Bryan came charging up behind Bonsworth and knocked him flying onto the floor, dropping the gun. Kevin followed, picking up the gun in his beak and running away from the floored farmer to find a place to get rid of the horrible weapon.

At that moment, Paulo's siblings also appeared. Gathering all their courage, they burst into action, charging towards the farmer with all the speed they could muster. Even Mittens the farmer's cat came running to help his new friends.

The farmer's eyes widened in surprise as the pigs swarmed around him, their squeals echoing through the night. For a moment, he seemed too stunned to react, his gaze darting around in confusion.

With loud squeals, growls and grunts, the group of animals dragged the speechless farmer into the barn and towards the pig pen.

Mr Bonsworth yelled in disbelief "Heeeeeeelp!"

All the animals worked together to get the farmer into the pig pen and dumped him in a huge pile of pig's poop next to the defeated and dazed Bruce the dog. The animals then turned and left the barn together. They all headed towards the clearing and in the direction of the forest.

With one last glance back at the farmer's house, they turned and ran, their hooves, paws and talons pounding against the earth as they fled into the safety of the woods. Behind them, they could hear the farmer's shouts growing fainter and fainter, as his threats faded into the night. With a sense of relief, the animals slowed their pace, their hearts pounding with exhilaration. They had done it. With Bryan and Paulo's plan, plus a little bit of luck, they had completed their mission. Operation 'Pigs Fly' had been achieved.

As they disappeared into the safety of the forest, Paulo couldn't help but feel a surge of gratitude towards the brave bear and cockerel who had helped them escape. They were finally free, and nothing could ever take that away from them.

Paulo looked up. "What now Bryan?"

Bryan smiled warmly. "Now we head back home to Branston Cave." There's room for all of you if you
would like.

Paulo had a cheeky grin on his face as he asked, "Operation homeward path?"

Bryan chuckled. "Operation homeward path in motion!"

All the animals cheered and celebrated as Bryan and Paulo led the quest. Along the way, Paulo couldn't help but steal glances at his siblings, their faces beamed with excitement and anticipation. For so long, they had been trapped and confined in the barn, their spirits crushed under the farmer's rule and using Bruce as his assistant in the pigs' downfall. But now, as they journeyed towards freedom, Paulo could see a newfound sense of hope flickering in their eyes, a spark of joy and liberation that filled him with pride. With Bryan's guidance and Kevin's unwavering support, they managed to overcome the odds and secure their freedom, forging a bond that would last a lifetime. As he drifted off to sleep, surrounded by the warmth and love of his family, Paulo knew that no matter what challenges lay ahead, they would face them together, as a united front against the forces of darkness. For in the heart of the forest, in between the towering trees and the whispering winds, they were heading not just to a place of refuge, but a home, a place where they could be truly free. It seemed like nothing could stop them now. With this perfect team, visions of great times loomed ahead.

However, back at the barn an angry farmer and his dog came back to their feet. "I can't believe those pesky varmints, this is now a state of war! Bruce, together we will take our revenge and hunt these thieves and traitors down. C'mon boy, we'll go back to the house for supplies and my guns and then we'll head out first sunlight. I'm gonna call cousin Elroy too, he's got more guns than the law. Plus, he's a wonderful tracker. It's huntin' season boy!

Bruce growled and grinned menacingly in reply.

Chapter 8
The Final Hunt

8

As dawn broke over the peaceful forest, the light filtering through the trees created a mosaic of gold and green. Paulo awoke to the sounds of nature, alongside his siblings who were feeling a sense of peace they hadn't known in a long time. Around him, his family and new friends stirred, getting ready for the day ahead.

Bryan greeted them with a warm smile. "Good morning, everyone, I hope you all had a wonderful sleep. We still have a long way to go to reach the cave, so we need to make sure we are prepared for our journey and get going."

Paulo stepped forward and looked around at the tired animals, just waking up. "You heard Bryan, let's check we have everything and then get moving."

As they packed their belongings and prepared to move on, Paulo was full of determination. They had come so far, and nothing would stop them now. He was sure. However, the feeling of unease still lingered in the back of his mind, a nagging sense of impending danger.

Back at the farm, Mr. Bonsworth and Bruce were

true to their word and planning their revenge. Armed and ready, the farmer stood beside his dog, his face set in a grim expression. He had a score to settle. This time, backup had arrived. Cousin Elroy, a burly man with a bushy beard and a reputation for his tracking skills, joined them, carrying an arsenal of weapons. Accompanied by a pack of hounds, he was ready for the hunt.

Mr Bonsworth stepped forward. "We're gonna find those animals Elroy, and make 'em pay! Let's move out!"

Cousin Elroy nodded, loading his rifle, and exposing his crooked yellow teeth with a grin. "Wooooh, let's round up some cattle!"

He grabbed a handful of hay from the pig's pen, holding it under the noses of his hounds. "Boys, get a whiff of this?"

The dogs sniffed eagerly, catching the scent, and a sharp whistle from Elroy sent them moving in unison, their noses to the ground. The hunt was on.

Meanwhile, deep in the forest, Paulo, Bryan, Kevin, and the others pressed forward, staying low as they moved through the dense trees and deeper into the forest. They stuck to the shadows and stayed alert for any signs of pursuit from behind them. They also took turns scouting ahead ensuring their path was clear and safe. Their goal was to get back to the cave as smoothly as possible and avoid any signs of trouble. Especially the dangers that Paulo and Bryan had narrowly escaped on their first journey to the farm.

"We need to stay vigilant, the farmer and his dog won't give up easily." Bryan advised quietly.

Paulo nodded, his eyes scanning the thick bushes around them.

The forest, although beautiful, felt like it was closing in, every rustle of leaf and snap of a twig, setting his nerves on edge. As night fell, they set up camp in a secluded grove. All the animals, especially the pigs, felt exhausted from the day's journey. They took turns keeping watch, the firelight casting flickering shadows on their faces. The forest, usually a place of peace, felt ominous and creepy. As Paulo sat by the fire, thoughts of what was coming raced through his mind.

He turned to Bryan. "Do you think they're close?"

Bryan shook his head, his eyes fixed on the darkness beyond the firelight. "I don't know, Paulo, but we must be ready for anything."

Although the night went by without incident, the tension in the air was clear. As dawn broke, the group quickly packed up and resumed their journey. Every step brought them closer to Branston Cave, but also more wary of the threat that followed behind them. As they neared the cave, the sounds of the forest seemed to grow quieter, as if holding its breath in anticipation. Bryan guided the group to a concealed entrance round the side of his cave, where a large rock blocked the way. With a grunt of effort, he pushed the rock aside, revealing a narrow passage that led into the main cavern.

"We are here," Bryan announced, his voice echoing off the stone walls. "It feels good to be home."

Paulo turned to the group. "Make yourselves comfortable guys, this is our new home, you can relax here."

The relief was clear as the group settled into their

new sanctuary. In the cave it was warm and welcoming, with a freshwater spring and ample space for everyone. For the first time in a long while, they all felt safe.

But unfortunately, for them, the feeling of safety was short-lived. Outside the cave, Mr. Bonsworth and his cousin Elroy closed in, the hounds leading them directly towards the cave. The scent of the animals was strong, and they knew they were getting close as the dogs started barking and growling.

Elroy smiled, "We're real close now, I can almost smell those critters myself."

"We're almost there," Bonsworth snarled. "Get ready, boys!"

Inside the cave, Bryan sensed the approaching danger.

"They're here," he said, his voice low and urgent. "We need to defend ourselves."
Paulo and his siblings, although scared, were ready to fight for their freedom.

Paulo stepped forward, his eyes blazing with

determination. He faced the group and spoke with fiery conviction. "We won't let them take us back!" he shouted, his voice loud and clear. "This is our home now, and we will defend it with everything we've got. I know you're scared. I am too. But we've lived under the shadow of this man for too long. He's hunted us, broken us, tried to take our lives away. Well, not today. Today, we fight back! No more running, no more hiding. We stand together, and we stand strong. This is our chance to be free! Let's show him we're not afraid anymore!"

As his words echoed through the cave, a wave of energy surged through the group igniting a spark in their hearts. The fear that had gripped them moments before began to loosen its hold. One by one, they stood taller, eyes burning with new confidence. A few started nodding, and soon, cheers erupted from the group.

"Yeah!" someone shouted. "Let's do this!"

"We're with you, Paulo!" another voice rang out. The cave filled with the sound of their rallying cries, their voices blending into one fierce roar of determination. It was a loud, defiant cry of unity. The group was ready. No longer just survivors, they were fighters ready to defend their freedom and their new home.

As the farmer and his men approached the cave entrance, Bryan and Kevin took up positions. They knew that a confrontation was coming and that it would take everything they had to win.

But they were not alone in their fight. Just as the confrontation was about to begin, a low growl echoed through the trees. Dera, the wolf, emerged from the shadows, her eyes shining with fierce determination. Her wolfpack spread out behind her, surrounding the entrance to the cave.

"You didn't think we'd let you face this alone, did you?" Dera said, her voice a reassuring growl.

Paulo's heart lifted at the sight of their allies. "Thank you, Dera. We could use the help."

The farmer and his cousin hesitated as they saw the wolves, their confidence wavering. Mr Bonsworth's grip tightened on his weapon. "What in tarnation? Bruce, sick 'em boy!"

Elroy barked an order at his dogs too. "Get 'em, boys!"

All the dogs charged at the animals growling and Mr. Bonsworth and cousin Elroy started to aim their weapons. But the animals were ready. With a fierce determination, they launched their counterattack, using the terrain to their advantage. Bryan's massive strength, Kevin's quick thinking and agility, the wolves' ferocity and the pigs' craziness, turned the tide in their favour.

The battle was fierce and chaotic and the air was thick with growls, barks, and shouts. The cave became a battleground, each corner filled with the sounds of desperation and fury. But the animals fought with everything they had, driven by their freedom and unwillingness to return to a life of captivity.

Dera and her pack moved like shadows, their lethal precision overwhelming the hunters. They struck in perfect unison, their coordinated attacks sending the enemy reeling. The hunters, skilled but disorganised in the face of such relentless fury, struggled to hold their ground.

Paulo and his siblings worked together, weaving between the attackers and charging at them relentlessly. They used the cave's narrow passages to their advantage, darting in and out. They were outmanoeuvring the hunters at every turn. The tide was turning. With every strike, every dodge, they pushed the intruders back further, gaining the upper hand.

But just as victory seemed within reach, Paulo found himself face-to-face with Mr. Bonsworth. The farmer's eyes were wild with fury as he scrambled to his feet, grabbing a fallen rifle. His face twisted with hatred, and he levelled the gun directly at Paulo's face. "This is all your fault!" Bonsworth snarled, his voice trembling with rage. "You think you can just take what's mine and run? You think you can defy me?"

His finger tightened on the trigger, his hand steady, ready to fire. Paulo froze, his heart pounding. Time seemed to slow as he stared down the barrel of the gun, unable to move.

"Times up Piggy, I'm gonna make sure you never see another sunrise, time to meet your maker!" Bonsworth spat.

But before the shot could ring out, Bryan lunged forward from the side with a roar of aggression. In a blur of motion, he slammed into Bonsworth, knocking him off balance. The rifle flew from the farmer's hands, clattering across the stone floor, as Bonsworth hit the ground hard.

Paulo gasped, stumbling back as Bryan stood protectively between him and the fallen farmer. Bonsworth glared up at them, winded and disarmed, the hatred still burning in his eyes, but his power over them had shattered. He got up and went for his gun, but with a final surge of strength, Bryan sent Bonsworth and Elroy sprawling back, their defeat clear. The hounds, sensing the battle was lost, whimpered and retreated with their tails between their legs. One by one, they quickly disappeared into the forest. Bonsworth and Elroy scampered to their feet and fled behind their retreating dogs.

The cave fell silent, the echoes of the battle fading. Breathing heavily, the animals regrouped, their hearts pounding with the thrill of victory. They had done it! They had defended their new home and secured their freedom. As the defeated hunters retreated, Bryan turned to Paulo and the others with a proud smile on his face. "We did it, we're safe now."

Paulo nodded, his heart swelling with gratitude and pride. They had faced incredible odds and emerged victorious. Their bond was now stronger than ever.

Dera stepped forward; her eyes were warm with approval. "You fought well, Paulo. You and your family have earned your place here."

Paulo smiled thankfully. "Thanks, Dera, but we couldn't have done it without everyone's help. Thanks so much to all of you!"

Bryan spoke up. "Thank you indeed. Now is anyone else hungry?"

All the animals cheered and celebrated. As they settled into their new home, the animals knew that their journey was far from over. But they also knew that together, they could overcome any challenge that came their way. With a sense of hope and determination, they looked towards the future, ready to face whatever adventures awaited them in their newfound freedom. As the sun set over the forest, they knew that no matter what happened, they would always have each other, and the strength of their unity and friendship would carry them through. And so, in the heart of the forest, amidst the towering trees and the whispering winds, they began a new chapter of their lives, filled with hope, courage, and the promise of a brighter tomorrow.

The End

Thank You

Thank you for reading my first book. I would love to hear any feedback you have whether good or bad. Please can you leave me an honest review when you get a chance. I am looking forward to writing you my next book.

Best Regards

Jolyon G.C Stevenson

J.Stevenson

Printed in Great Britain
by Amazon